Iowa Legacy

By Diane De Vaul

WEP Poetry Series #3
1979

Acknowledgments:
Some of the poems published here appeared previously in the following magazines: *Aleph*, *Black Box*, *The Mill*, *Phoebe*, *Poet and Critic*.

"Nasturtiums" received the Dellwood Citation Award, 1978.

Typesetting for this work was made possible through the assistance of the Writer's Center and the National Endowment for the arts.

Cover photograph by Mary Clare Powell.

Published by:
White Ewe Press
P.O. Box 996
Adelphi, Md. 20783

For Fred Klein

Wall-Eyed Pike

Wall-eyed
pike
motionless under the dock,
becomes a shadow
slender in the weeds

by day
soundless.
By night
it jumps
and announces
with the slap
of a tail
as simply as that
the separation
of form
in what is
one long
intercourse
fish and element.

How many of us
announce
that separation
so clearly
so cleanly?

Roots

I got caught playing
in the dirt again
examining myself for roots.
I couldn't find any
not even a fragile
hairy one
starting from my knee.
I tried rubbing
soft dirt
against the warmest
wettest part of me
but it would not sprout.
That's when someone came along
and offered me an apple seed
which I took
of course
with my lips
(my fingers still smelled
of promise).
I planted it
and overnight
it sprang up
a gnarled tree
with deep roots
and many knots.

I sat in it
naked
and stroked it
with the softness of my body
tried to fit its knots.
It was a soft spring
and the tree seemed
to like me.
In the fall it died
and left my yard
tangled with its half
submerged roots,
that tripped me when I
tried to walk at night
and embarrassed me
in front of my friends
by continuing to grow
without a trunk
or fruit
or leaves.

I Want You

I want you
like I want
a hundred blackbirds
to somersault
down a snow soft hill
with eyes crackling
tongue chattering,
white feathering
red and black,
to somersault me lightly
out of winter
into spring.

I want you
deep beneath
the city
in the raw tunnels dug
and hollowed out
to receive the thrust
of metro's coming.
I want you there
on a warm spring night
in the underbelly
of the city
to have you
with the earth smells
the rough wood timbers
and the rumble of traffic overhead.

Hidden in a fold
of Montrose Park
blocked by
incessant pacing
of city streets
I want you
high
in a Tulip tree
raising your vision
with the fiber of your limbs
the sensuousness of your leaves
unafraid to flower
and litter the ground
with your seed.

A Response To McLuhan's Mechanical Bride

A knock on the door.
Another salesman,
a disposable white hatter.
He comes in
unfolds
his Stetson
adjusts for the tilt of his head.
He sniffs around
sizes me up.
"Look," he says
stepping forward
"let's get something straight
between us."
"You'll have to straighten it
out yourself," I say
backing up.
"I plumb my depths,
you scale your heights."
(I love cliches.)
He slumps in a chair
opens his case.
"How much of a man
could you use?
A head, a good front,
right arm,"
then he pulls it out.

''Part of a hand
two fingers worth
could attach a third
resilient but soft.
Feel it,'' he says.
''Now this isn't your
ordinary model
note the special device
sensitive to heat and wet
mini computer to
select optimum tack
spring-loaded rotary action
instant feedback
optional rerun
programmed in.
And once it gets a hold
it never lets go.
Get it,'' he says winking,
''You can't turn it off.
It's compact,
goes with pants,
recharge monthly,
what do you say,
pardner,
Happy Trails?''

"Inside The Blood Factory"

I feel the knot tighten
inside, anger
pulling at my knuckles
snapping them in place.
I'm tired of the whine
of the blue Wakoski,
the little girl
concentrating all her attention
on the hoop that goes
rolling off.
She spends her days
locked in a sand box
playing marbles
with the hard
excrement of her father's
neglect.
Sylvia Plath,
Anne Sexton,
do you think you win
flinging your death
in your father's face?
The seed
they planted in your mouth
is death
and you nurture it
and play with it
like a child.

For Sally

My love
with its blue shadows
lies like broken limbs
over your house.
You carry the ocean
depths in your small body
sailing over it
with mocking eyes.
Your hands know
the sureness of a bird
flying home
against an orange sun.
You dance your body
nostrils flared
daring men
to ride you.
At night I hear
you spitting your challenge
running under the moon
body sleek and hot as a lynx
after the kill.
I am afraid
of losing you
half wild
and untamed as you are.

Fifty-Minute Fantasy

Naked in a white raincoat
with peacock feathers
fingering
my ass,
breasts painted with
the fragrance
of flowers,
my navel
encircled with flashes
of red and orange
spirals
that run down and around
to lick up the other side
curving over haunches
and sliding down my thighs,
I throw my coat away.
I perch on
your bookshelf
and weave my siren song
around the others,
their ears stopped
with wax.
Invisible to all but you
I spread my thighs
and coax the spirals
into flight.
Riding their flashes
I drop down on
the top of your chair.

You,
unable to escape,
except in studied indifference
(bound to fifty minutes)
I hold your head
between my legs
and feel the
rubbed smooth
of your face
melt and run
against my thighs.
I sing through your hair
breathe fire in your ear
and lick out the flames.
Curling up small
in the bunches of your neck
I dive down
your back
and come up
like a sleek mink
between your legs,
brush soft
your cock hard
with breasts and belly.
Then when you
open your mouth
in surprise
I slip in
and feel your hollow
with a blind hand.

Under the cover
of your clothes'
darkness
I sport along
your limbs
to shinny
down your trunk
and sit
in your crotch
and ride you
with the wildness
wind stirs in trees.

Nasturtiums

Nasturtiums
burn orange
under the cover of
summer squash.
Day lilies lean
from the woods
toward the road
throats on fire.
Black-eyed Susans
brazen with
their private suns
and velvet shade
stand in the center
of the highway
demanding to be seen.
I pick from each
a part of myself.

Words

Tonight I gather
all my words
and climb
the stairs,
find the roof
that oaks
top with ease
yet high enough
as I stand at the edge
to feel my death
come winging in.
I send them off,
these words,
domestic pigeons,
off to do an eagle's
flight.
They forget
as soon as I let them
go. On their own
they perch
in the trees
wait to be
called home.

The Man Following Me

A man is following me
older, in a black turtleneck
he takes a seat
to my left
and slightly in the shadows.
He does not smile
or look at me.
This is the third
restaurant I've been to.
I reach for another cigarette.
I am weary of running.
Sometimes I go over
to him, once took
him to a loft
in an old barn
near a creek,
made love to him
until the sky
fell through the cracks
in my eyes
and the stars
rained down the roof.
I never learned his name.
He follows me still
but refuses to go
again to the barn.

If I Had It My Way

If I had it my way
you'd give me two weeks.
I'd lock you up for one.
I'd never leave you alone.
I'd molest you when
you brushed your teeth.
I'd tie your pants in knots
and work on your toes
and I wouldn't quit.
I'd hide under your pillow
and slip my tongue in
your ear when you tried to sleep.
I would come in your dreams
day and night
black cat in heat
kneading your body with small paws
my tail tickling your nose.
I would lick you
lick you
until you bellowed.
Then I would soothe you
with my fur.
If you tried to escape
I would trip you
fight you
fuck you
until you gave in
and the second week
I would have it my way
which is every way
I could think of having you.

For Fred II.

I always run in patterns,
squares
to cubes,
into abstraction
and out any
available ear.
I run with purpose
being lean and moral
and if I run over
some people
it's because of pictures
painted on my eyes.

And I hit a wall.
That wall is you.
At first you simply
insist
I dump the sand
out of my tennis shoes
so I can run
without gritting my teeth.
Then you suggest I
run in circles
so I can see you once a week.
You put up mirrors.
The clothes come off
next time around
and in the end
it is obvious that it
is just me
running
the lines on my face.
You laugh in relief
when I stop
and walk into
my life.

Iowa Legacy

There is a place where the road
slides down
the smooth curve of the land
into a tangled crotch
where trees cling stubbornly
and a river winds beneath the brush
rioting in the summer heat.
Hidden from the road
a farm house decays.
I go back
leading my horse a long way in
along ruts that mound and swell
around the narrows
running through grass grown tall.
Rabbit paths sneak off
through tangled raspberry
and indolent songs weave
in and out of the wind.
Among the shadows of the oaks
I stop and tie him,
strip off my clothes,
throw back my head,
shake loose my hair.
Beginning with his head
I brush and curry him,
down the neck
through his thick mane,
down the sloping withers
and over the short back,
until his coat shimmers
a black silk.

I let him nuzzle my thighs
and nibble them
with the warmth of his muzzle
while I play with his ears.
Head leaning against his flank,
I stroke the inside soft
of his haunches,
touch his sheath
as he tenses and kicks.
Then I jump on,
wrap my legs around his neck
and laying on my stomach
over his back
feel the light sweat
of his body along mine,
reach under his belly
to stroke him more,
finding him unprotected,
until he snorts and stamps
and fights the rope that holds him,
throwing his head up against my thighs.
The heat of our bodies mixes and merges.
The warmth and wetness
moves through us in a dance.
I sit up trembling,
then laughing,
turn around,
unsnap the lead,
and give him his head.
He leaps and bucks,
then we're crashing into the woods,
leaping the rotten timber,
the fallen trees.
I cling to his neck
as we break through the branches,
my legs slipping back over his sides.

Seeing the river ahead
I feel him gather,
the brief hesitation,
and the cool darkness of the river
draws me closer.
Snorting and blowing
he takes the other side.
Cantering now,
rhythmically dancing,
he pulls up, controlled
beneath me.
Holding him tight with my legs,
I let go of his neck,
close my eyes,
blend the rhythm of my body
to his,
and let my sound go
the soft moon of my body rise.
No longer able to hold back
I throw back my head
cry out
and dig with my heels.
The surge and madness of power
blacken my world
and for an instant
I fall tumbling through holes.
Then I bury my head in his mane
and let him carry me back.
Spent
I rest in the tall grass
while the sweat dries on his flanks
and he grazes
contented and calm.

To My Brother

Listen — quiet
your heart and listen
they are running again.
Their hoof beats
are racing my heart
wild as
they take the years
in stride
barely lengthening
their reach
flashing whites
of their eyes against
black sky.
The wind sweeps
the night of my body
reminds me
with its force
of how deeply
I love you
the one who raced
those nightmares
under the terror of
those dark skies
with me even when
we were alone.